THE MAN WITH HIS BACK TO THE ROOM

Selected Poems 2000 / 2005

Other titles by Roger Aplon:

Stiletto
By Dawn's Early Light at 120 Miles Per Hour
It's Mother's Day
Barcelona Diary

THE MAN WITH HIS BACK TO THE ROOM

Selected Poems 2000 / 2005

ROGER APLON

A collaboration from Barracuda Press and Barcelona Custom Books

First Published 2006 by Barracuda Press
in collaboration with Barcelona Custom Books

ISBN:0-9651329-2-7

Copies of this book have been registered at the Library of Congress
Aplon, Roger
Selected Poems.

Printed and Bound in the United States by
Bookmasters Inc.

Book Design by Jane Darroch Riley
Cover Image © Kim Sohee

For Judy

who coaxed me back

& special thanks to Ed Smallfield for lending his keen eye & ear & editorial expertise

I From Daybooks

II In A City You've Painted Black

III The Man With His Back To The Room

IV The Woman In The Window

V Concert w/ Laundry & Lemon Tree

I

From: Daybooks

May 31, 2000

She stands at the window & smokes & the ash lengthens on her cigarette but she doesn't notice & stares down at the street that is slick from the morning rain & sees the traffic & hears the horns & smokes & the ash falls on her gown but she doesn't notice & leaves the window & walks to her bedroom & puts out her cigarette & removes her clothes & stops to light another & walks to the bath & takes a moment to relieve herself & puts out her cigarette & steps into the shower & runs the water a bit cool this being June & already a warm film has settled over the city & she washes away her agitation but not her dream from last night in which she swam out too far & could not breathe & the hands that held her pinched & prodded & now she runs the water colder & rinses what is left down the drain & steps out onto her shiny white floor & wraps herself in a towel & lights another cigarette & exhales into the mirror that tells her not to drink her scotch into the early hours & not to eat her fill of chocolate & she turns back to the room with only one window & sits & looks out on the city which has become calmer & more ordered & lights another cigarette from the last & crosses her legs & smokes.

From: Daybooks – 1999-2002

July 9, 2000

She wears a scar that curves from her lip across her cheek to her ear.
She was cut by a man who found her home &

when she smiles (which is rare) it rises like another mouth &
puckers like it would open & speak &

when she runs (which is often) her features tense & her new mouth
glows like a wire – hot & powerful &

she wears one glass eye on a thong around her neck to see in the
dark & a needle taped to her leg &

she flies a black flag with a man's face at its center & has etched
a red welt on its cheek & the number 6 between its eyes &

at the end of her street she's painted a door in the eight foot wall &
when she must, she opens it & runs through &

down the hill to the river & to the ship that carries her back
to the beginning.

From: Daybooks – 1999-2002

October 14, 2000

For Tom & Jennifer

Travelers on the wing & time to spare & a meal in store. "Fill Up Here" reads the sign at Cafeteria José i Maria where we drop our duffels & portable gizmos & relax over a plate of spinach & wild mushrooms & down a glass or two of Torremilanos from Ribero del Duero & catch the eye of a painter from Santa Monica who knows a haunt or two & offers coffee at his studio . . .

I've come to the gate & knocked three times & spread his ashes as he asked &

I've planted sage & thyme & mint at the base of the fountain in the yard & asked forgiveness &

I've been drenched in the rain of days on the road & learned to savor a bitter tongue & lime &

I've listened to the ramblings of men at the alter who rub against each other & kiss &

I've seen the women too who handle their sister's bodies like their own & lick an ear & tongue &

I've weathered the coast in an open boat & fished for my dinner in coves & gullies & killed &

now I ask to be left alone to steal a dream or two for myself / hollow out a small place under these fading stars.

From: Daybooks – 1999-2002

October 22, 2000

The river repeats & repeats & repeats & up the mountain & down
like a rush of skin & blood & bone & voices
lost ...

1
Bite Down! Bite! Me! My face, My breast, My cock, all the tender parts. BITE! . . . & the mouth opens & remembers & nurtures & births these memories &

his face all suds & soap to wash away pain & what we have left are the relics: grandparents off the boat & parents with their gentle care, the first dance & the first love, the naked truth at fourteen & fifteen & the new love with her horse & the wedding & . . .

2
The mountain recedes & there's the remnant of flesh alive & folded in & over the bodies & over her & over him a knot of hair & an arm but no face to lead the way.

3
I will cover myself in honey & invite the flies & bees & I will not move as they fight over me & eat away my skin.

4
I've written all I know or want or care for on my body & have marked my heart 'rouge' for you to find your way.

After: The poses & postures of the artist **Zhang Huan**

From: daybooks – 1999-2002

December 28, 2001

Marrakesh, Morocco

They wrap a green snake around my neck & one reaches into my pocket & the other whispers his love in my ear.

These men smell of olives & garlic & sage & will do anything for money. They smoke hashish & drink sweet mint tea &

send young boys to fetch tourists to their stalls where they wait with a bone & a razor & a smile to charm a donkey.

I sit with them cross-legged & stoned & watch their soft soled shoes shuffle through the bazaar &

while the charmer plays his flute for the cobra the others shuttle closer across their boards of nails & this river of hot coals.

From: Daybooks – 1999-2002

A Dressing Gown

It may have once embraced the moist & perfumed skin of a Japanese Geisha as she plucked the strings of her Samisen & sang praises to her prince . . . It

may have served as the leisure robe of a dark-eyed Tahitian goddess as she tempted the passions of a lusty sailor from Lisbon or Marseilles . . . Its green

satin sheen may have once graced the long lean body of a fiery courtesan from Barcelona or Paris or Marrakesh . . . &

who will know & who will come to tell.

Today it hangs in the privacy of my bedroom where my lover comes to treat me to her unique & eager style of love &

when she lets it slip *Oh* so slowly from her shapely shoulders it colors my dreams with its red & yellow peacocks & pheasants & soaring hawks &

as she straddles my mouth & treats my lips to her exposed sex I hear the peacocks scream & feel the hawk's breath in my ear & it's then

I roll her on her back & ride into the night remembering the light & tawny lovers of the earth & the dreams each has shared with each.

From: Daybooks – 1999-2002

II

In A City You've Painted Black

but there's one with fast water & mountains & cars that hold the road as if I might complete some trip

as if destiny were a fact & all we need do is be there like a giraffe needs tall trees & it

seems to play well unless the torrent is swift & logs & dead cattle & here's where a bend comes in handy

& a quick swim to the other side & a bonfire & someone hands me a cocktail with a cherry in it & my old friend Dave is laughing

with a new girl on his arm & invites me to take a break & I do going faster than we should down that

mountain road when the lights of the town come into view & there's a fire at city hall & a patrol poking

their noses in our windows wanting us to explain which we can't or wont or don't in time & they chase us

toward the river & the careening cattle & David jumps with his love & I steer into oncoming

lights before I'm clear of debris & wanting to get back to my dinner but can't find the way &

the last I see are the stains on my pants & the need for a bath & no one I know is in the room & my cocktail is warm & the cherry . . .

No matter how little you care, it will suck you up / hound you
with mayhem & massacres. It will slice your feet,

shit in your sink, eventually . . . blow up your car. For the time
it takes to wheedle its way into

your ear, crawl up your ass & churn your guts, you'll be its
audience. In its hands you'll be

driven to scuttle time . . . flounder through sewers . . . together,
you'll be treated fairly, together,

you'll be driven from gutter to gutter, outflow to outflow . . . From
end to end & side to side you'll wallow

in discontent . . . witness boils & the last star of the night . . . You'll
be lectured on absolute conviction, cautioned against

repetition, told tales of wolves released in raw tundra. Starved
for conversation, you'll lose your

sense of time: Monday will become a basking walrus while
Wednesday carves a satyr's mask from the hip of an ox.

In the beginning,

you may find yourself intrigued, encouraged by changing seasons.
You'll volunteer for research, offer to wrestle buffalo, sign on the
dotted line.

In time, you may think you're in charge, begin to give orders, ask
for a raise. You'll think you can rearrange destiny until, without

provocation, it'll stop you in your tracks & sober you up with a
word or a quick spike to the neck.

I tell you this with no illusions / you were never one to be
advised or warned of a slack step.   Last winter,

you ate well at its expense / this year, you must watch your back,
surround yourself with fire, never reveal your eyes.

Enter & be teased   *Enter & be soothed*   *Enter & discard your eyes*

"In many ways, I have become my father's object of desire.
It was not planned & neither of us willed it so."

If you must, remember Cancun & a hot ride in the bush.
We were together for the first time in years . . .

"We showered in separate rooms. He'd sent flowers. No.
Someone had sent flowers."

He was handsome in his white slacks & tight blue shirt
with the name of his rowing club & I, slim & tan in a fitted
sarong . . .

"I've read of events very close to these & did not believe them.
Maybe you will know me better if I tell you . . . "

Can't you see us dancing? It was so innocent & she was
there too
ordering drinks & tipping the band &

"When I was certain, I caught the first plane. What more could I
do?!
But . . . today . . . "

Should I order something special or plain? He'll want me
to be impressed. Should I ask about her? Will he . . .

to herself dreaming.

The Aging American returns to Avenue Mac Mahon

> *"It's so elegant," she whispers, meaning The Arc De Triumph & The Eiffel Tower & The Louvre or was it what she meant . . . it's been so long . . . so many years. ..*

The Tuileries simmer this warm spring day & Parisians by thousands grab a chair & turn into the sun

& the same is true in Saint-Germain-des-Pres & along the Champs-Elysees & the Luxembourg Gardens &

in fact, the city revels in this release from winter & even the tourists move more easily to each of their private visitations:

"If Pigalle's your sporting turf, so be it," says a wily cabbie & I'm reminded of another time & a stroll down Avenue Mac Mahon

carrying my head in my hand & dodging gendarmes & the sweet aroma of her sweat & mine in the floor above the concierge &

bathing in the sink or not at all & goldfish dead in their soup & a pond of steaming swans & clipping each other's toenails &

if I wouldn't leave, she did, all the way to Cleveland, Ohio & a lawyer she used to fuck on the sly & this time the buses leave on time &

the room has a shower & Ellen & what more could you ask in May with a toasted crepe in one hand & a cold glass of a ripe & ready crisp Sancerre?

Lately,

I've been climbing over sweaty bodies for a better seat at the
Bareback Express

when the elevator failed & we all tumbled / Gwen over Patrice & me
back to beginnings

where all you had to carry in your kit was a ticket to ride & a bindle
of glue or skag or you'd get left

sifting through the garbage behind the scene / courting Suzy Q
who's all decked out

in ribbons white & ribbons blue / hair the color of seaweed over one
ear &   that magic

nipple oozing Cutty on the rocks // & lately I've been trying to get
back to wonderland with

both hands on the throttle as if I were an engineer out for one last big
ride with pearls &

petticoats & rot gut by the gallon // I can see it clearly now /
Johnny's gals can-can /

naked as beaver . . . every thatch a twitter with each thrust of a high
spiked heel

& me rounding the corner for one last look before the curtain comes
down & Billy

The Bouncer tags me one for old times sake & the band strikes up
Desolation Road

& the crowd goes wild drowning out the screams from the back room
        where Terri's

turning up the heat & there's hell to pay & say, did I tell you the one
        about Jan & The Dealer

where you can't trust anyone to provide a clear picture of drowning
        in the wake

of a lost love straying to the sidelines as the last Big Red Bus leaves
        with her head

in the lap of some common crook crooking his fingers for me to see
        one by one

with each wig & wag of the wiper blade before it's around the corner
        & out of sight &

as if for the last time or the last chance / you might say / for good
        and good riddance

if I weren't sober for the first time in five years & it didn't hurt so much.

My Friends Have Been Having An Adulterous Affair

He's been needing a tart surprise & she's a model craving a wider
lens & when someone offered him a martini she ate the olive &

when he dipped his brush in the red oil she bent-over-backwards
preparing a smile & swallowing hard &

he stopped smoking & knelt for communion & ate the body &
remembered how long it had been between meals &

she launched a few balls in the air to jiggle & juggle & no one
tossed in the towel or shut down the oven &

their goose burst its skin & his stuffing flew & grapes he'd been
grafting & her pickled tongue &

in this reel they move across sand growing smaller & into the trees
& pop-up full-faced & grinning & slightly distorted &

in the next, she's pregnant or just pretending with a puppy under
her coat to suckle her breast with its thick nipple &

wisps of dark hair & in the last frame she shows her naked ass as
if this is the end or is it the beginning &

out of camera range, she takes her shot of Lemon-Hart while he
tries his luck at the family's antique nickel slots.

Orphaned

He wonders where he's been all these years & cannot sleep but walks these hills like a general addressing his troops in French & his children in Spanish &

when we first met he spoke English with a stutter & talked of his childhood as if he were on a train that had no number & no name but served elegant meals &

each evening at eight he'll dine alone at his desk in the library & wash down his repast with a dark Rioja or Rhone or Cabernet & when he smiles you must not mention his teeth

or the scar that runs like a laser down his cheek or the howling in the vines . . . but he will confess he's never at home in his house & has frightened the cats that come

to feed on the chickens & mice & he'll tell you to be wary & lock your door & escape while you can before the rain has erased your name.

Almonds

. . . each seed an eye . . . or is it the shape . . . of an eye . . .

If you squint you may see many in the shape of almonds but none so tough . .

1

She sits on his right & does not glance one way or the other & her sister sits on his left & neither have spoken for years but they attend to him &

their eyes glisten in the day & highlight the night like beacons or torches or bonfires lacing the hills.

2

In the orchard, between each tree, someone has planted a flag & someone has buried their mother's ashes & another – a silver spoon . .

In April, when the fear of frost has passed, he digs down & turns up a wedding band &

a bundle of bones the roots have grown around & a tin & a weathered certificate they could not read . . .

Oranges

I've been thinking of oranges & lemons & . . . cigars & I've wanted a cool orange to suck on a hot afternoon & here it is winter & a hot cigar too &

be careful to roll the skin back slowly or it will crack & your design will fail & don't choke on your smoke & . . .

he'll be coming soon & his mastiff will mark his way & he'll wait in the trees at the end of the road & you'll smell lemons & oranges &

see the smoke from his pipe & you'll dream of a river to be crossed & a bucket to pull from the well & a cup &

he'll kiss you & you'll inhale his breath & he'll lead you off with his pack of dogs &

you'll notice she's scented the air with oranges & stirs your lemonade with sure strokes & adds just enough vodka & mint &

while you drink she'll massage your neck with her hot hands & peel away any doubts & your shirt & she'll offer a cup of ashes & leaves &

the three of you will hold hands & read from the cup & lie back to watch the clouds & listen for the one dog left to hunt alone . . .

She always relished the first big reds of May. Would rub them over her bread as they did in Gerona when she was a girl &

garlic & oil & salads in winter with green & tart & a *Sofrito* she slathered on spinach to make it sweet &

crawling on hand & knee in her grandfather's garden to find the ripest under the vines & peeling them &

scooping out seeds & building her first *pasta con tomate y pesto* for Niko her Italian &

well chilled *Gaspacho* for Gabrielle her Spaniard & fried for her mother who calmed their heat with a cool *alioli* & the ripest

she'd squeeze to a *bota* & pack her case & ride with you to a cool spring where you'd swim with her under the willows & lie down with her

in the cool grass & tear the bread & spread the ripened cheese & fill your mouth with juice / its ages / green & white & pink & red.

Olives

'Plant trees for your children & the fruit will come for theirs . . .'

A young herder plays his flute & his leader her jangling bell & in the olive groves the trees are full & soon, before the ripest begin to fall, the women will come & spread the cloths & the young men will climb out where they can & shake the tree & loose the rest & rush to the press & that night the pungent oil . . .

Greens & black & gray & pink & purple & cracked & whole & pitted & stuffed &

cured with onions & garlic & peppers hot & peppers sweet & thyme & dill & tarragon &

sampled with breads from Barcelona & cheeses from Pamplona & a cool glass of Fino from Jerez &

the oil you'll drizzle on ripe tomatoes & onions & anchovies & toasted baguettes & this you'll serve in the shade

of a misty August afternoon as the families gather & the kids race to soccer & the women shuffle & riffle the cards &

grandfathers stare like pilots into the distance for that perfect place to land . . .

1 – The Souks: day

The boy with fire in his eye & the quick hands of a thief shuttles us beyond the chickens & lame donkeys to see how wood is seduced from a block to a box & lacquered & inlaid with silver & stone &

copper is twisted & bent & scored & etched & polished &

the tattooed hands of women & roasted dates that hum against the gums & snakes that bite & monkeys & Iguanas that do not . . . &

mint tea & honey cakes & a single carpet sixty feet across &

deep in the interior on a darkened street we're led to the peddler of bones who dances his fingers across a board shuttling skulls & knuckles & toes down the alleys of my life which throb & narrow & glow . . .

2 – The Souks: night

Men. & the aroma of roasting meat & fish fried crisp & boiling pots of broth & cous-cous piled high with diced tomatoes & roasted eggplant & chicken & almonds & onions &

Men. Eager & jostling & eyeing the foreign women who've come to see & the air thickens & the air stiffens &

a dozen lanterns create pockets of light where young boys box for money & musicians & singers & some stop for a meal & some for a sweet & the menu is the same & the menu is different &

Men . . . call you to 'Come' & 'Sit' & 'Taste' & chanting & drumming & you may be tossed from your place & whirled around or running

the dark streets where cars & carts converge & you cannot breathe & cannot remove your mask but dance to the drum with your caftan stained & beard askew & a thin chain that glistens on your neck & . .
Men . . .

From the dark side of this hand-turned jug come fish & the hooks that took them & their mouths

are flared to let them breathe & their scales are bruised & they seem to weep & their tears run white along the black &

the hands that brought them here have made their mark – a thumbprint, a nail, an . . . open palm / &

there's the head of a goat in a bowl with one good eye that seems to contemplate our curiosity & the scent of honeysuckle &

lime & an octopus whose eight arms straddle his collapsing home – a half-peeled potato – gray skin tracking a run-a-way ball . . .

. . . an elephant squished & squeezed & bent into itself until all that remains is the trunk & half the head & buzzards &

crayfish from the lagoon & the odor of dung & a papaya perfectly split with seeds intact & a rosy glow &

a pyramid of skull on gnarled skull fractured & scattered from watering hole to watering hole to river to stream . . .

these skulls & bones &
nothing ever wasted . . .

Night – Carrer Sant Pau

The street is Carrer Sant Pau & it leads to the bar Marsella where a small boy sits in a chair & prods me to buy his pipe that he'll fill with his special mix of Asia & Africa & he slips between the slivers of light & is back with a jar & I strike a match & the band plays softly at first & louder & the boy is gone & his mother comes & lays out her cards & I'm told I have to choose & I take the red road & she leads me back to America & a dog I ran from & a girl I kissed in the basement & my mother who always behaved & my father who hid his stained collar like a sore & then I chose the blue road & she took me back to Alicia & a night in Marrakesh when the breeze blew hot off the desert & I heard the tapping of camels & she knew how to apply tea to a burn & her lips to a swelling & after that I chose the black road & the peddlers of knives & potions & I bought one of each & ran ahead & heard my own voice in my ear & stopped & asked for the last & she opened her hand & in her palm lay a silver key & I took it & asked her to come & we danced & she left a lily in my lapel & I smiled at her decision & turned away & went on.

July 27, 2000

'The Door of No Return' is etched in stone & stitched to the eye of time

. . . the mystery of *'the disappeared'* . . . before Argentina – before Chile before . . . America.

A father would sell his daughter or his son or the wife of his brother to another

Chattel: blood & bone & muscle & skin & . . . the meat of men & women on the run

herded & shackled & stunned & dumped behind 'The Door of No Return' . . . "Am I not my brother's keeper?" &

he would sell his brother & uncle & aunt & his mother if she be fit & there's the neighbor too . . . & the shaman prays & dances &

they come in the night & bargain & by first light the ships have sailed & row on row of ebony flesh shimmers & shines & the light goes out

behind 'The Door of No Return' where the Governor opens the woman & rides inside & leaves a boy or girl to be raised for God's good work &

it's cold & it's hot & there's no bucket for your shit & no bread & no honey & no milk & . . . & for the herder & his sheep

there's no escape.

From: Daybooks – 1999-2002

May 14, 2000

Venice - Rome 2000

1

" . . . our memories are your only grave."
December 5, 1943 / August 17, 1944

When the Venetians were asked to give up their Jews, they refused & the Reich demanded & soon a few & later more & the tablets testify of the gatherings & of the deaths

2
They haven't yet called for the girl . . .

preoccupied & wrestling / one hooks his arm across the throat of a lion & wrenches his mouth wide /

another hugs like a bear & hauls the huge torso of his rival to the ground & when they do

. . . she must recant her god & when she wont they slit here throat.

3

On the train to Rome.

acres of tires & smoke & tented rows of tomatoes & church spires & one inch of rousing dark coffee & rain & Bologna & white ducks & freight yards & graffiti & black & yellow cranes & she knits a multicolored scarf & mountains & banks of white roses & purple iris & red poppies & the Orient Express with pink lamp shades & mist & long tunnels & bright blue headstones . . .

From: Daybooks – 1999-200

In Sierra Leone the intruders cut off her hands & his arms & her legs & they cut & left & in the chaos that is the hospital for the disabled all the appendages have escaped incineration & march or crawl or stutter or stagger like an army weathering winter but not in Sierra Leone . . . it is too hot in Sierra Leone . . . Here – they march like an army drenched in sweat & blood that leaks from their ruptured veins & they hunt in the bush & the back-streets & alleys for 'Junior' who did the cutting & wore his name plainly & with pride & his eyes glowed & his machete & he spoke mumbo-jumbo & preached freedom & peace & butchered & left this young girl, no more than fifteen years, to be fed & cleaned & used by the merciful or those who are not.

will notice his skin that their fires have charred & you will see his nose is not . . . but a plastic snout & wires & his ears no longer & no texture but a yellow waxen shine &

you will notice her stumps where there once were hands that could sew & stir the pot & stroke a young boy's face & you may note her silence but will never ask, "What have they done with her tongue."

After: Kosovo 1999

After Octavio Paz

You whisper like the blast of a whip, like a woman's scream in the dark, like the stink of shit / you toss your grenades &

I'm here with outstretched hands willing to hunt like a hawk, like hornets, like angry bees.

I'm the kid in the back-seat who wills you gone, the dancer with only one good leg, a monkey on a string who sings Aida . . . &

here you take my hand & hers & twirl her like a top & catch her in your lap like an unwise lover *I hear your kisses / watch*

the rise & fall of your haunch & I ask again, "Take me under your wing, teach me to fly without eyes & hear without ears & live without hope."

Lean Boy on the Beach

His choice. A boy to parade for his pleasure. & now there are a gang of boys & they swarm over him & tear away his camera & rip his clothes & leave him in a heap at the side of the road that leads to the sea.

Heat . . . Heat that sucks moisture from the sand & air that undulates & lifts & leaves a thin film on the skin

. . . & surf to channel a bridge to the other cove where they lie & face the sky / arms tossed & hands that touch & stroke & go limp . . .

They posed for him & danced for him & stripped for him & took his money & whisky & rolled away on their boards &

one would stay . . . usually . . . one would stay.

It was whispered loud enough for us to hear & when the whispering stopped I could hear the music through the walls &

the steady rhythm of their fucking & once in a while I'd hear him whisper again, "Do It!" "Do It Now!" & he would say,

"I won't without him." "Not without him too." & the music would stop & there was nothing more to speak about.

After a Photograph by Herbert List

of swollen rivers & lives dismissed like branded dogs, I've come to drink your tears, to intrude on your perfect fog. There's

a butcher, red vest open to the sun, knife in one hand, basket of bull's balls in the other. I order mine with mustard &

there's Audrey with her yellow teeth & skin like putty who offers to wipe my slate clean & pours a cup of Darjeeling & whispers your name

as if it could bring you back whole: Josie . . . *shush* . . . Josie . . . & there's a gunner in green fatigues nursing a baby &

a naked dancer spread-eagled on the kitchen table pulsing open & close the lips of her vagina & Henry the florist holding

a wreath of carnations & iris & lilies & a banner which reads: **Smoke One For Her Sake . . .**

In this country there are men dusting off their eyes for one last look & drinking urine & cursing the dark &

runners who turn downhill to avoid rain & a conductor tempting fate & stirring a restless pot of gunpowder & beans &

masked men who open their faces at midnight & women in the upstairs rooms who fiddle & sing & rub glass in their wounds.

In Pursuit (of grief)

My father had little use for poems, less use for the future...

"Provenance"

Joe Stroud

1

My father died alone, shot so full of morphine he couldn't care his wife had left his options to the docs & I, home on holiday, went to work dismantling a life file case by dresser drawer until all that remained was the gavel from his Masonic lodge & his ashes that I declined to scatter . . .

& when the crematorium called & inquired, 'What's to be done with the box?' I asked it be dropped at sea, you know, tossed from a plane or however it's done & when they seemed perturbed I'd not take charge I lied a bit & said, "It's what he'd expect."

2

Today, when I pass a neatly ordered field of corn or beans or tomatoes, there's usually a man behind a plow or hoe or walking down the rows & stooping to pick something, put it to his mouth & taste its flesh to know how it's going & how it's going to be in the end when he'll finish what he started.

The arms that wave from the windows are black & the cats that roam the street are black & there are black beards & black hands & black market toys & you've blackened the windows & shut my eyes & locked my door & painted a black X on my back & when they come to claim their prize you feed them black bread & black beans & black rice & lift the black iron pan & toss your black mushrooms & black butter & when I reach out to make you stop you drown me in the black rain that falls from your thick red wound.

where hollyhocks no longer bloom & engines run amuck & the view
of your mountain is lost to time. I've come

with arms full of nettles & burrs & briars stuck to my leggings where
a blue boar nurses the gypsy kids & eats their enemies whole.

I've seen it gnaw the leg of an insolent peasant & the face of a county
cop & I've slept in its den & washed its feet & combed its stinking hair.

There's not much time or so they've told me & I want a drink of clear
water & a taste of ginger on my tongue.

Teach me to sleep again & teach me to hold on with both my hands
– there's a home long deserted & no one to turn the key.

III

The Man With His Back To The Room

Confluence

For Dian & Judy

On the ride north we reminisce about family ties & kids on trial & growing up estranged & how discovery can set us free &

where three rivers converge there's the constant & submissive sea to welcome & absorb the sludge & sap of continents &

where the monument to Lewis & Clark celebrates challenge & risk we're encouraged to contemplate transcendence & what it takes

to map mountains & lakes from the bow of a birchbark canoe & how the yowl of a hungry Grisly pawing the air in spring might churn the blood &

how some men assume futility but insist on going on & when the time is right accept the Salmon's challenge & swim upstream to spawn & die.

Astoria, Oregon – November 29, 2002

Rock, Water & Wood

For Dian Greenwood

White water for a mile or more & tidelands flecked with black stones & trunks of lost trees & towers rise from the surf & mist & a lone fisherman with a gnarled hand & a wet pup & kids with castles in their buckets & streams & moats & a riderless horse appears at the edge of the land & four feral dogs & the sun runs behind clouds & a girl's haunting song from a subterranean cave all glitter & light with starfish & crab & the beach is deserted & the tide swells & the tide runs & the dark horse gallops into the surf & the driven dogs & the sun appears all ruddy & warm & the cliff's awash in foam & the thick tentacles of kelp & a hand rises from a root & a face from a rock & the howling of a wolf & the steady drum of wave on wave on wave holds the land transfixed & damp with its ominous kiss.

Canon Beach, Oregon
Thanksgiving 2002

The Man With His Back To The Room

There's a fly combing its furry legs & just below the window a mannequin with hard white tits lifts her head to speak.

There's **Public Parking** in black & gold & the reflected vision of a lamp in the soft lap of a naked dancer. & now

a wave crests above the man with his back to the room / above a dog asleep under his chin & the doctor

loads morphine & mucous & a rubber tube filled with grease & a guitarist strikes the wrong cord &

you've come from the mountain to refill your cartridge casings & stop for a bottle & the familiar stroke from a tired Bob . . . Bob

whose brother sits with his back to the room contemplates a run for the border & a night with Elizabeth &

he reminisces: an afternoon in Tokyo with a Siberian husky & Joyce who held the mirror & brought sushi . . . that afternoon in Muskegon:

a bride & a quick twist behind the barn . . . & it's here the man with his back to the room turns & knows

you're always alone with your own memories & sees your thick tongue & blood on your hands.

It was easy to down that first footloose flagon
running through trees & sun-bleached hollows
dancing to drummers in dark cantinas where
the booze was hot & that young girl with
whiskey breath & sweat stained breasts
took me to her mother's bed &
that thick, intoxicating cream
she rubbed into my skin &
that morning on the train
to Vera Cruz & the port
& monkeys in cages &
young boys who beat
each other blind for
nickels & dimes &
the tall, rich albino
painter in Madrid &
the story of the leap
that transported him
to a blue grotto & a new
life where memory is blank &
the deeds of the past are swallowed &
the next years are filled with the ornaments &
trappings of a stranger in purple robes & no one left
to remove the blood from the sheets or the body from the room.

. . . But Fighting There / Is One Ray Of Sunlight . . .

. . . & without it's eternal flare there would remain only the recognition of your brutality, the knowledge of a gesture so cruel as to bring down a black dark from which there could be no escape.

I'm not through grieving. No! But,
I come to these days aware of new growth:
relish intercourse again & lobster bisque & a mellow Monte Christo.

I'm not through grieving. No! But, have willed myself to wonder aloud,
bask in a warm breeze & the red finch's song, listen again
to Coltrane's blues without tears.

I sort my days for evidence of a small precious stone that I might lift
like a tiny lamp to lead me out & into that ray of sunlight
that is there / fighting with the dark.

After: the poems of ***Miguel Hernandez***

Someone will arrive soon carrying a bouquet of black roses & they'll ask for a number only you'll have memorized.

Don't run to the first priest or minister you see . . . he'll deny the present & sell you the future instead.

There'll be nights filled with tigers & doctors in green gowns – there'll not always be time to choose.

We speak so casually about starvation . . . like the parasites who hide their heat, sort their loses & wail under iron cots.

Remember. A young girl with red curls walks her greyhound every day at five. She'll need your help.

Relish these passions like nipples to be sucked. Bask in the surprise of a hot February day & pretend there'll always be another train.

In Some Circles

In some circles she'd have her own chauffeur a seat at table topaz & emeralds &

someone would polish her red shoes & walk her Basenji & curl her nails & pour her drinks &

there would be actors to play her parts & actresses to fondle her breasts & a blind singer or two &

once in awhile a dark man will come & she'll wonder why & when he's gone she'll hide his scent &

swim between their roots to the end of the oaks & gargle with his blood & shoot billiards in the basement &

sneak a peak at her master's cocoon & here she'll plant her toes in loam & wait

for the next jet to land & the next ship to stop at their dock & open it's arms & she'll take you back &

milk you like a goat & mold you into loaves & come to the end with her eyes on fire & her mouth nibbling her knuckles & moaning your name.

faces float from her blue tile floor: An Aztec warrior in full battle
dress leaping through fire, a wizened chess champ

surveying a field of unblinking eyes // In the corner, a long
feathered bird cradles an entire ballroom in its outstretched wings,
rats

gnaw at a wooden puzzle of the world // There are multicolored
candy canes & water that falls on naked bodies;

flabby men & flabby women smoking black Galoises. There's a
bearded barber reading a Portuguese racing form, two

adolescent girls rolling marijuana & grinning at the photographer
she's hidden behind a green silk screen.

Against the far wall, a blizzard of white chalk-dust obscures a herd of
galloping ponies / in the distance, scored & bleeding bodies line a hill &

in the sky above a fleet of fighter-bombers / their flags disguised.

The Man In The Mirror

The man in the mirror hangs a ladder from his narrow perch
in anticipation of attack.

His famous somersaults have always been smooth with only one
catastrophe mentioned.

The man in the mirror has seen a face behind his own & now
knows there will be others watching.

On the night in question, he pays a woman to teach him her
body & is interrupted by an aging acquaintance.

They speak openly of death & transition & the woman overhears
& pastes her worn-out portrait beside his own.

That was June when the cut was fresh, tissue soft & no scar
where now a black welt rims the place that will not heal.

In The American West 1979-1984

This is not the American West of John Wayne or Warner brothers, No! This is the Amerika of John Lynch & Count Dracul . . . of Richard Avedon: This moneyed wise-guy who's come to snap the simple folks on the plains . . . to make an irritating image – *How did he survive their rage?* ***I guess we'll never know for sure?!***

Eyes. You fix on the eyes: Black faced coal miners who stare down his lens. Their whites the only reflected light.

Beads of black sweat on a furrowed face in Eagle Pass, Texas / slick & sticky blotched skin of Oklahoma Oil.

White / Scaled / Gesso miners / Cody, Wyoming.

These images, too reticent to speak, squint or smirk or curse / Are mute / Are mutant / Are – at war with Avedon: Accuse – Suspect – Accuse.

They've been conned before / maybe by the best / maybe by his 'Clarence Lippard' *drifter Sparks, Nevada,*

by the playful nonchalance of 'Carl Hoefert' *card sharp, Reno, Nevada* or maybe

they've been plagued by Syphilis or Gonorrhea in Salmon, Idaho or lost their teeth in Albuquerque, New Mexico or / been scorched by radiation in Rocky Ford, CO.

These men & women are not the talk of cocktails or stuffed quail in New York City – No! But, we agree, this is Avedon's country too, **Damn You!**

& when, like a ripe egg, these Great Plains part, the dead will carry the living into battle & on each front you'll see their eyes first:

vacant & white & running blood.

Richard Avedon: Photographic Portraits
– Caxia Forum: Fundacio "La Caxia"

(God has given you a gift & a whip to wield with grace)

The woman who squats at the edge of the village is the wife of the Shaman & the decapitated head she births (its mouth sewn shut to retain its soul) is that of a warrior won in battle & now (as they tell us) it will join a shrine to the ancestors of her husband & all who march in the wake of history.

It's been a dry year. Even the sorghum wilts
as if in prayer.

While the Shaman tends his wife
husbands dance & stutter
from one foot
t'other.

The head, when it's released, is greased with the gloss
of her mature scent & its spiny headdress
has drawn blood

passing, as it does,
through her vaginal canal

its eyes blind &
lips chapped &
a tongue
gone green.

Where does the 'soul-matter, reside?' one murmurs? It's the
'soul-matter' that counts here.

Isn't it?

As the hunters would have it?

Isn't it?

For this we risk our lives too,
to bring him back &
seal his head
between her
majesty's
legs?

*****

What will become of our harvest – you can see it's already flat & without steam?

& our pigs & goats & my wife's third-born – coming soon – what of him?

Maybe we should have eaten the heart as it used to be or the muscle of the thigh – my father spoke of that.

There was tradition then & what of . . .
His voice trails off. Something unsaid. We will not know.

Maybe it's the cock we should have saved or the . . . *he too stumbles his words barely audible from his stitched mouth.*

We were assured it was the head & now it may be too late to find what's left.

When he fell he knew what we would have – as if it were our own, as if we could impart the same powers to the earth.

It's here the Shaman appears & drags a long stick through the dirt. He holds tight to the braid & waves the dripping skull above his own. He chants his mother's famous song of pleasure & survival & birth & death & how the body rushes to claim the earth & the earth the body . . . &

*****

It's now past sundown.

Some have drifted back to camp while others sit to sip their wine or beer, but, all watch, either

from the grove or from the windows of their homes / watch & wait & sniff

for the first signs of the promise . . .

That promise given with conviction, with that air of certainty, with love.

The promise of the prized & the inevitable, of clouds that hover & those that pass.

The promise of impending trust & envy lost.

The promise of a cleansing & of healing & of faith.

The promise of the storm that will surely come, where, in the soot & slime,

an orchid climbs.

. . . at the base of the Sycamore . . . as if it were spring.

As if your mother had opened her arms.
As if dad still ruminated on his war & who was left & who was not.

As if it were summer

& we played capture the flag & Johnny drowned rescuing a cat in that whirlpool of stink & blood.

There's no turning back from that or the second lie where the posse gathers to hunt you down & in the dark.

They ride & you're away,

trapped in your liar's roost / out of the arc / out of the bed / into the light where the saddled stallion stands & stomps / sweat

on his haunches / neck aflame with the juice of battles won & battles lost & it's here the devil rider comes

from the saloon & in time to join the flood & the first showers of September

pepper the dust at his feet like tiny gunshots / Ratta-tat-tat – from the hidden side of his eternity, from the hidden side of his soul or

whatever he calls his shuffling, rambling frame,
referring to a past he'd rather not know & a future he'd rather avoid.

It's always been like this / it's always been / him / waiting with wings loose & the inevitable darkness . . . &

it's here he whispers to her one last time:

___________________(*fill in the blank*) – the movie is yours – or not.

the woman dreams of a winter night / at home in a tropical cave / a snow leopard asleep at her feet / sun through fine ferns that coat the walls / a Toucan perched in the Teak tree.

It's then she feels a throbbing between her legs as if something unmanageable had entered her & from the back of the cave the voice of her lover who disappeared years ago calls her to hurry or

they'll be late to the carnival where she finds herself in the arms of a stranger with a black beard & gentle hands who strokes her belly & slips something under her gown & now she walks on the edge of a cliff

an uncomfortable sea below & a desert spread out behind & for a moment she thinks to leap from the cliff but turns instead & runs to the dark where the sand is hot & the wind too &

large hoofed animals stride at her side & she feels a thick fluid escape her body and stream down her legs & when she looks she sees nudibranchs & anemone & hears the whistling of whales &

in the distance a blue crystal pillar she knows she must reach & it's there she comes to rest & for the first time in her recollected life feels overcome with an unexpected sense of bewilderment & joy.

Dance I – Tango in Two Parts

Fold back the sheet & find her naked / in Tango / with a man in a white suit & wide-brimmed white hat & a cigarette dangles from his thin lips & she seems startled as he slips his hand lower on her back . . . & see

the orchestra is led by a bearded man with bare breasts or is it a woman with a beard (who can tell from here) & as he manipulates her closer to the open door we glimpse his driver below who waits with the wide black car.

Close the sheet now & see them dance over the garden wall & down the dark path where the driver has brought the car & see him lift her & twirl her over his back & see her laugh & wrap her legs around his head &

watch now / the tango partner cracks the whip & has them strut like bears stuttering in the moonlight – like squirrels racing their tails – like orphaned acrobats tearing out their arms & beating back the air.

Dance II – Tango in Two Parts

In the backstreets of Montevideo there's a woman who tangos all night with the bus driver & the barber & the bartender & as she holds them close she licks their blood from her many small incisions.

At first light they follow her home to her flat above the bakery & she lets them, one by one, come into her arms & kiss her thick red lips & leave their sultry scent & with that – the last they will remember of their given names.

The Man In The Gray Hat

"I'm the first office in the house of love; call me desire"

From: An ancient Greek erotic drawing

The man in the gray hat

has a pawn ticket in his pocket & a memory of suicide.
In winter he carries a gun & news of religious sacrifice.

In spring he'll rescue his camera & shoot down his latest
budding affair.

It will be construed as murder by his psychiatrist.

This is not the first town he has lived in but the street-signs
know him & whisper of a rendezvous with her & revenge.

Last winter he wrote his last will & testament &
last summer he wrote another & . . .

I can't tell you more / this is all that's left:

A pacing tiger. A sliced cantaloupe.
$12.00. His wife's death certificate.

& this inscription:

Desire Will Triumph

Gracia – Night – Living Out History

The widows gather at Placa de la Virreina to sip their
brandy & coffee & evoke the years since '36 & lovers,

sons & husbands swept away by the furor that was Spain.

It's spring & there's jazz in the street but no one moves.
Even the football game, Barca & Madrid, head to head, can't intrude.

These crones keep vigil / day & night /exacting memories.

No one left to insist, no one to nurture this weathered flesh, no
bounty paid for what never was & will never be again. Just

down the booze & shuffle home to the cat or croak – who cares.

What We Will Not Know (of Torture)

When I first met Jamie & Beth they were swimming in the river we all called Styx.
You know.
The one keeps us from walking round with the dead.
Well.
For a while.
Anyway.

It begins with grumbling
like the grinding of granite knobs
a hammering & battering of steel plates &
the crack of a whip & bones snapping or a slug to the jaw &

bombs & rifle fire &
the smothered bodies sliced &
diced & spit back between the iron ribs
that separate those behind the screen from the rest of us.

& the klieg lights come up & into your eyes to search the back of your head for a brain unsprung.

& the knuckle-wrenching climb to the wire that's wired to the generator that's wired to the dam that spikes

like heroin its electric charge to the veins.

& before the night begins again there's the unmistakable bitter-sweet scent of shit & the rank stink of toasted flesh & the sweat of fear &

& hole is cut in the tongue of one young enough to be your grand-daughter & a thin, barbed chain is dragged though that hole & her blood is collected in an urn that's delivered to the priest that placed her here & there's the smell of her roasting at the foot of the god-head that holds success as a gift & failure as the exception.

& the one who the soldiers desire is forced into the room saved for that purpose & when they've divided her between them often & as they please she's tossed to the hogs that surround this place & . . . & when it's quiet again there's the small, wet sound of whimpering & on the screen an enlarged hand is displayed while one by one its nails are extracted & a mouth where one by one teeth are or have been & . . .

a man tethered to a chain is dragged though the slime that is the blood of his comrades &

a scissors is rammed up his ass & another & a cut is made & another & one at a time & then by hundreds &

the cage is a door & the door is a cage & a wall & the gurney is wheeled through the yard &

bodies are tossed in the pit & the drivers arrive & the drivers go & . . .

the kidnapped & the captured are led away to wait for the night & the knife & the glare &

the wounded to crawl & the river to rise & the sirens to cease

& the mocking . . .

When I last saw Jamie & Beth they were floating in the river we all called Styx.
You know.
The one that's supposed to keep us from walking around with the dead & deranged.
Well.
For as long as we're willing.
Anyway.

After: **Herrumbre** (Rust) – Compania Nacional de Danza – **Nacho Duato:** Coreografia
Body and Cosmos: The Sculptural Art of Pre-Columbian Mexico – **The Rituals**

Barcelona #21 – September 17, 2002

I hear the engines of the Boeing 767 moan in the night & know this was not a mistake, this, erecting a plan for the alternative:

I'm reminded of Grace & her twin sisters, the ones with the birthmark in the shape of a butterfly at the nape of their neck.

They would often be found at the edge of town with a sack of rice playing at marriage to the donkey or the dog &

I remember her borrowing candles & an Indonesian prayer wheel she'd whirl over their heads & chant

the song about flying to the mountain where she'd begin another life as an actor playing the part of Jezebel & how

she'd send her sisters to bed with a razor & wait for the morning & the grief they would bring to the family. This, I remember now but

when I board the waiting plane all that is past & the next time I see this place I will have been born in the likeness of a climber

who sees the top & never looks down.

For Bernard Rudden

we'll build your mother a temple where she can assemble dolls that glow in the dark / whittle teeth from jasper & fingers from tourmaline.

When the rains come again we'll be halfway home & weep with the kids who run red in their own blood...for stallions left to rot in fouled stalls.

After the first snow I'll uncoil a length of rope & hang the first man who enters our house & opens his case & dares to sell the remnants of stars.

When you move to another city I'll bury Simon under the house, nail your last song to that old Oak & with a thin heart I'll leave too...

stop on the canyon's rim / let loose the doves.

IV

The Woman In The Window

Cairo

1

The outskirts of Cairo are unfamiliar & deserted before the sun has broached its crumbling rooftops but as we slow for the rail crossing we see the man who smokes his cigar in the upper reaches of the orange tree & the speckled chickens that roost in the doctor's eaves.

There's a broad stand of corn that shimmers in the wind like a legion of lancers marshaled to guard the women who scrub their pots in the Nile & the young girl in the blue pleated skirt who polishes her glass & the boy who fishes & the dark sailor who reaches into the wind.

Many houses have had their stories scalped by landlords & where flowers grew the untended plots are home to goats & a few sunning snakes & where the lovers might lie under the stars there are only feral cats to greet the stranger in search of tea & a place to rest.

2

The desert crawls / the desert barks / the desert bathes in a squalor of dreams

There're no bare-bellied dancers to entice the sphinx & no singers to coax the reticent mummies. No. This caravan limps between the slender legs & elongated torsos of the ones who come in pairs led by a man in a feathered cape & a woman with child & a barren woman.

In the night the sleeper remembers the battle hymn of his lost brigade & charges the gate with his gun cocked & his shoes untied. There's evidence of poison in his glass & the corpse of a weasel hangs in his closet. This is not an excuse. These are facts to chew on.

In Cairo the camel drivers roll dice & smoke & eye the tourist dollies & the bored snake charmers swap CD's & spike their mint tea with gin & in front of the old hotel a river of sentries & when the bomb explodes, as surely it must, the senator will read the last page & close the door.

Confused in the metro the young girl with haunting breasts & a cane hobbles to the map with a pregnant girl who claims to speak several languages. They

surface outside the deserted bullring with its aura & odor of a blood-sport lost & without a beat they stop to kiss – it's a long thick kiss &

as they mount the steps to the blue crane that straddles the river & a block of dead houses they turn into the wind & remember

all that has passed through their lives & at the edge of the roof the girl who carries a baby tosses a ring & the other a book & a map

of bridges crossed & they both toss their lists of names & photos of dead parents & now the pregnant one hurls her unborn &

presses her flat belly to make sure & the last they throw are their own birthdays & the masks they've worn with pride &

when the camera pans back we see them float away on a barge filled with lilac & phlox & as they round the bend downstream we notice

there is no bird left to guide them.

He Fumbles With His Banana

When I bothered to look / I found my father's body gone / where he'd hid himself
Paul Auster's Memoir: The Invention of Solitude

It's been years & there's no longer a mention of the old man.
Just a melody or two. Time has eroded my memory. And his.

There's a hint of too much solitude: a flattened tire, soiled linen,
rusted pots & pans, a memoir half explored.

In the bureau, under the socks, I find a suggestion of romance, that
simple quest gone wrong . . . & you'll ask, why not shuttle these remains

to the junk heap? Why have the nesters been allowed to smoke his
favorite cigars, dilute his collection of pornographic postcards?

When the question of fertility arose, he'd stuff a banana in his
jeans, march to the liquor cabinet & drown another day

just like the last. If the burden were his and his alone, we'd
certainly forgive, toss out expectations, wonder aloud

how the seasons seem to pass more quickly, turn off his tapes &
make a date to begin.

After: Colum Banus' presentation of Samuel Beckett's Krapp's Last Tape – Barcelona – 2003

like a finger through flame as if one mistake will take him back to the beginning where fire swept away all notion of home & remnants of a life once lived as if in dream where (in slow motion) her body falls through air & her eyes stare into a future he will never know & . . . & here he stops to appraise the view from the cabin door & the smoke in the distance & the shuffle of the herd & now he steps away for the first wolves & again for the seer with his compass & sword & now he dissects & sets aside the possibilities of romance in the spring & a cat to curl at his feet & another mountain in the distance & a river & a valley & one last look & now its time to close the door & set the lock & strike the last match.

How Far We've Come

Light dims on the marchers who cross the plateau to the oasis, where the last falcon lives & the alligator & a pair of ocelots asleep in the weeds.

They make no sound, these men who march in single file

into the heat of the desert, into the womb of the present gone berserk, into the spleen of death . . . to the belly of hell itself.

They're joined by the men & women from the valley, all who remain of the river's kin. They come empty handed & in silence;

trailing cannon, carts & carriages,

past a corral where the last elephant lies dying in the dust & a derelict bus where the skeletons have been stacked.

They're followed by a blind dog & a boy who offers them pears.

They pass a herd of gazelles gnawing stubble & a cemetery & a mud-hole where a lone tortoise sleeps & dreams of rain.

Their leader wears a dried heart on a gold chain.

They've been taught to look away & never touch.
There will be no conceptions.

It is understood.

Ask the oysterman in the blue vest & stained red hat. He knows the tides & where to find a sturdy ship.

Ask the young whore who already knows your body. She will open a tube of silk & lead it into you.

Ask the dark one who has stopped to plant his seeds. He carries an ivory knife & knows the caves.

Ask the cook who bastes her leg with red wine & herbs. She will write you letters that only speak of rain.

If you can catch him, ask the one with the tapping shoes & musical feet. He carries magic cards & is never afraid.

Ask the conductor who caresses his violins. He'll open the sky & read you the stars.

Out Of The Dark

I speak of that place where a mystery will not be solved, where the suspects speak in tongues & cannot look each other in the eye,

where the deck is always stacked against the players & no one to catch the fallen.

I speak of a rendezvous with the hanged man who suggests a shovel & the guard who demands retribution for night sweats &

will suck the last breath from those who were sent for help but disappeared in a bottle.

I speak of Baby Huey & Charley D. lost on the last step of the last landing, eyes rolled back, the needle stuck & dangling.

I speak for Ellen dead of her own hand the 38 still cushioned in her collapsed lap.

I speak out of the dark where light is only contrast: the outline of times past, a hint of a future that could or may be. I speak

from the place that stirs a thousand pleas: for a door, a tunnel, a stick of bone to lift the rock,

any thing or any way to stop the drumming in the ears, the stuttering hands, to finally escape the blinded mind.

At the city dump,

this oily mist makes the day as dark as the night that will come soon as they dig for that last rotten fig or the wormy apple or a maggoty bone.

Their kids are most active; diving here & losing their footing & sliding in the slime & grunge & carrying off the prized pieces of gristle & sinew & fat.

Underground

It seems like underground. The drifter comes to her for solace & a kiss & she turns away & looks to the floor where a roach scurries & now

he goes to the man who scratches his leg & bleeds & scratches his face & bleeds & scratches his arm & his neck & leers at her but will not speak to him & . . . &

At The Shore

it's another who's come to lay out her eggs – all two thousand – cracked, one at a time, until the beach is full & swimming in eggs &

the tide rises & sweeps away the first & back they come & the second & the third goes out & back & all two thousand yolks & the tide rises &...&

She Eats Her Onion,

gnawing through its pale skin, gnawing the bitter & the sweet, the juicy & the sparse & as she gnaws she drools & bites the air &

tells the story of being herself & the large size of her breasts & the too large size of her ass & the size of her long nose without complaint &

whatever she needs she will have & as she gnaws she talks of what is expected & how & what she will not & spits & bites the air & eats . . .

& now the eggs are whipped in the waves & go on to the next life without a life & lie in the froth & foam & bear witness &

the garbage mound is rank & the garbage mound is rancid & the harvesters shuffle to the beat of their hunger & their fallen pride & dig & sort & . . . &

even now, no one will speak out & no one will touch the other & the onion eater sneers & the onion eater jokes & she is not afraid & will eat another &

bites the air & grins.

Passing Through Fog

. . . we leave behind three or four images of ourselves, each one different from the others; we see them through the fog of the past, like portraits of our different ages.
Chateaubriand

If you turn left at the first roundabout & follow the road for a mile you'll come to the cemetery where she holds court.

There's a sweetwater spring on the property & a large brown cow in the shed giving milk; the boundaries are clear.

She came first for the body & insisted it be a man's; dark & lean with a hint of muscle in every move.

Orange for the gown was her next choice but soon was convinced blue might & then it was magenta until yellow & . . .

Her skin may sag but her eyes are bright & she wields her scythe with guts & precision & startles the mob with her wrath.

Will she know you now that the winds have changed & you're surrounded by empty trucks & an army of talkers?

Be careful what you pack in the night & heft by day; an alligator, two jackals – a monkey with sharp green teeth.

No one will hold you hostage in summer but in the fall there are many who need work; avail yourself of my services.

If you've forgotten I'll remind you & besides, somewhere down the road there'll be signs to follow, just like the last time.

The streets of El Raval

swell with the scent of Paprika (sweet) & Paprika (hot) & clove & nutmeg & cinnamon & rosemary & basil & thyme &

Jasmine Tea & mint & mango & bright candied tangerines & oranges & plums & melons & cherries &

we scoop them out & bite & find them not-too-sweet but full of the essence & drama of their kind.

This is the day we relish a rendezvous in a shaded plaza with a cigar & tea & a glance down an empty street

where the shards of Roman walls align the centuries & graffiti tells the truth of many yesterdays & today's

"No a la Guerra," & ***"No Blood For Oil,"*** is writ large for the senators & generals who do not listen &

these herbs & sweets are offered up as reminders of the covenant wherein the hungry are fed more than promises &

the wealthy will parcel out their excess & the great turtle too / may be urged, once again, to call us home, once again, &

balance our fragile world on its broad back . . . once again.

Easter Week in Reus

We climb the hill in a stiff wind to see Muntaner's '*Pere Mata,*' hospital for the insane, where, at its entrance, a slim athletic girl lifts up

in flight on a fragile wing of cloth . . . & from the window of our descending bus, we watch the tortured walk of a small black dog,

how he hobbles across the lawn & we stop for a drink in the *Plaza of Baskets* proffered in the hands of three naked nymphs &

the bronzed boy with a herd of geese in the next & we're lured by the stalwart & the suffering . . . inside the Church of Purified Blood

a woman bends to the bound body of Jesus, God of the Jews, & weeps & kisses his wounds & weeps & the drums begin &

the enactment of his walk & Roman soldiers in red & gold & hooded brothers in black & the wail of horns &

column by column they disappear down one street to appear in the next until the night is filled with their wandering & wine

flows like blood in the road & we shuffle along to be a part & suckle the scent of almonds &

leave a wish in place of grace.

The Anonymous Visitor

arrives & like footfalls in the night can erase all sense of calm

Like a dark hand that reaches through the door for the morning news or eyes

that track the subtle gyrations of your sister's tender ass as she boards the bus or stoops to pick a lily or

the long arm of the swimmer who stroke by stroke can cross unnoticed into you dreams & . . . &

there are those who are welcome & gone as quickly & those who disappear in a fog of junk & bad gin &

those who remain nameless & leave a finger or tooth or a cock that twitches at the slightest hint of skin &

lips that do not kiss & hands to wrench an eye from its socket or dive under the ribs to rip out a beating heart &

they'll tell you I've come to shit on your flag & demand I leave & if I don't there's hell to pay & the hole they've dug will be filled

without a trace.

the lights have dimmed & we bend to a movement in the wings & her
muscular body as it rotates slowly toward our introduction / & here

she tumbles to the stage & writhes & undulates & wriggles from her
skin & in & out of the backlit dark & the blood

that flows from her mouth & between her breasts pools in her lap
where the head of a cobra hisses & snaps &

as she sweats she casts a track across the Cyprus planks & secretes a
scent of lemon & rum & . . . &

the night hints at renewal & offers to erase the bitter taste under her
tongue & when her thrashing stops

she climbs to the top of the wall where she cuts the ancient cord &
it's here she turns into the light &

waves the red flag to declare a muted truce & I accept her terms &
promise (for now)

I will not follow.

& out pops his tongue like the blade it wants to be & cranes its vicious little head & clowns & crows & . . . & what

drives this thing, this soft puppet of a thing – this cudgel, this dowel, this savage urge to flex

between her legs like a godly rod & bob against the little knob she's raised for him to dart & toy about & tease & dive & . . . &

a sample here & a tweaking there & like an orphan unwilling to settle for nothing less but . . . But

what of its fine honed edge & the randy-dandy nature of its hurly-burly bird of lickerish & a radiant romp &

what of its itch to fly to that exquisite spot & plunder & gorge & disappear as quickly as it came & leave not a trace but

a quick dodge as swift as the camera's lens & no print but the one that flits from that face of the raging wife to the sorry horse – No!

Not this emblem of taste & savvy. No. Not this reward for what is not but could well be. No. Let us live in peace with it.

Let us warm to its measure & let us measure its prowess & its nose & its splintered edge & of course, this way, there'll be no myth but a fact to prove

& no one left but those it's lulled & bitten & tasted & sent to witness the coming &

the second coming too.

The old gondolier looks interested in the lady from Spain with her one black braid tailing down her back & sandals of Turkish leather & one blue eye & one a deep dark brown.

She, however, seems interested in the man in black with his white felt hat & polished alligator boots & a thin cigar that smells of incense & honey & smiles from under his brim.

But, true to his task, the gondolier steers them to the stop most requested & follows her with his eyes to the Basilica di San Marco where they disappear among the pilgrims who've come to be blessed &

the gondolier remembers another time when he was young & a woman from Greece arrived to be carried to her family at the Rialto bridge but left her card in his hand & whispered in his ear &

that night in the alcove under her stair they tasted the salts of the day that had glossed their skin & drank the musk they'd carried, one to the other, for that last ride in the Venice dark.

Welcome to Bosch's world:
Hieronymus Bosch, the painter of your nightmares & mine – a world ready for retooling &

Fabre's mentor on the mall of lost souls: where worms devour the flesh of the living & the dead &

assholes stride into fire on two legs & blue squirrels wear the heads of antelope &

the stomach as a cauldron steaming man-headed fish & bats flap from the vaginas of virgins &

painted on the sides of the barns we pass in the day "Copenhagen" & "Hoover" & "Coca-Cola" &

urine runs from the wounds & blood from the urethra & Jan will piss in her mouth & she will piss in the pool &

his game of 'one after one & two after two' is to be played the way we spin the bottle or dance or yo-yo / up & down /

where death stands at the door, his pistol in one hand & cigar in the other, where pools are dense with human shit &

orange trees shroud the timid senators who speak in tongues & ride the backs of geeks in iron masks &

so it goes in the houses of Bosch's hell & so it goes in the drawing-rooms of the well-placed & well-scripted –

those with wide streams to fish & bathtubs free of lice & women who speak with forked tongues & issue jelly-beans instead of love & lies

where truth cannot multiply or ever own the day.

*After: a quote from **Jan Fabre** (Un artiste et le sculpteur de la Belgique - 2003)*

this painting has her one full breast a bit too high & sprung from a
mat of hair & a kid in her arms whose lips miss the teat by an inch.

& when we look again it's not a woman but a man with this
misplaced breast who bears the baby in his weathered hands / more

like a weight he must endure than a creature to comfort . . . & the
figure in black who hovers at his shoulder / fumbles

with his robes & dares the painter to finish soon – before they're
caught at their suspicious game . . . In fact

these men glower as they approach – as if from a wake or furious
fight which they've won but, cut to the bone, have

claimed their prize – the child in swaddling who must be fed at
any cost & the breast is readied & thick with milk & leaps

from this princely chest – his victory at hand – his honor – possibly
upheld.

Seville, Spain 1999-2000

Here are the pictures – here are the rhythms & here is how they work:

1

He's asleep & the dream jogs without warning & he's in the street
& sound's down / motion stops & there's a rustling

among cast-off tires & bottle shards & cans & it's 1959 & a party at
Eleanor's & in the door walks Bob with his usual entourage &

the Big Car is waiting in the living-room stuffed with gardenias & a black
dog hunkers in the corner gnawing the remains of a blue-bodied bird &

three girls play backgammon & each roll of the dice illuminates the
pennies that fall from a dying constellation &

down the runway comes a ruffled satin doll with Tom Ford on her
elbow & a crow pecks at an eyeball with blood in its beak &

in the basement pit the McQueen brothers beat each other's
sweating bodies each blow a caress . . . each caress a blow.

2

There's a blind beige horse nibbling the neck of the drummer.
A boy with no arms holds its reins in his teeth & a wreath of lilies
& roses &

When I come for the water there is only shale, sand, a machete & .
. . a woman with no eyes.

3

It will soon be three years & no word.
As consolation they've offered their youngest daughter & two goats.
We each carry our own mess-kits, fish & tackle.

If it is to be / as it always' been / we won't need a guide
we will trust the river.
Remember me to those who wander & never know home.

I remember the photo of my mother & father on their wedding day. It was preserved as a statuette, the photo pasted on a Bakelite form & stood somewhere, I've forgotten, in the house on Cornell Avenue & later, I think, was stored in a box with other questionable relics.

In These Antique Photos

well coifed & indomitable couples appear inseparable. He seated. She standing. At his right. Straight & true on this their wedding day.

& the hand-turned & sculpted silver rings & gold that glisten & glow in the dim light have no facsimiles – each is distinct & only for the one it was chosen.

To Begin The Dance

she appears from behind the silver screen & points the way to her release & follows it where it takes her &

she's pleased with that & dances where the air is fresh & there are no conflicts & limits & no restrictions.

He Comes Next

proud of his fancy ways & poses & dances too & is sure she will take him in & she might but . . . not quite yet / not before

they duel & tease & tussle & tumble & confront their need to decide who will lead & who will not & who . . .

The Men Have Gone On

& the women are left to tell their tales & pose for the last time under the umbrella of their daughter's lens.
Their aging has a way of drawing them out. They speak directly & are willingly naked to the eye & to the unsuspecting ear.

He Dances Naked Now

& alone & refuses to be deterred & she appears & they continue their rhythmic dialogue – hand to hand & back to back & cheek to cheek & on & on

until they no longer know who they are but have become what the other was – he in her dress – she in his suit &

In The End

they make a bond – a decision not joined in haste & when it was decided is unclear & how they arrived together is a mystery

& what of the women in the eaves who stand beside empty chairs & will not show themselves without their ancient rings & new teeth &

what of those who do not sleep & can only watch from the frosted windows & will never forget the possibilities?

After: Reservat Per A Dones (Elsa Plaza- Pintures - Imma Gibert – Joies)
& Kleidenschaften (Dance) Janet Ruhl – Arnd Muller
La Casa Elizalde – Barcelona – March 5, 2003

Time Reveals Truth

She wears the map of her history stenciled to her belly & small
drawings of her ancestors silhouette her

young breasts & each time she is threatened by those who would
have her silenced

they're beaten back by the one who winds the clock & has been
her guardian since she was born & . . . & now

he cuts red flowers to send downstream & white to line the trail &
summons the bearers

to carry her to the mountain where she will give birth & when it
is right he'll call her to return

& reveal what we have never heard but must finally be told
if we are to go on.

*After: a painting by **Theodor van Thulden** & the photographs of **Tatiana Parcero***

This Is A Story Someone Is Trying To Remember

After Valerie & Ed Smallfield

If I can,

I will tell you of the deer dying in the yard & starved pullets
that wander in circles in the snow &

how I need to find the place they scattered my father's bones &
to hear my mother's final words.

If I ever can,

I will tell you again of my need to caress my first wife & not be thinking, 'Would Gloria take me back as I was.'

When I remember,

I might tell you volumes of lies that disguise faces & florid afternoons with wine & sesame cakes & visits from . . . but

chances are slim & the train will leave soon & before I go I wish you well &

warn you of the blizzard that will come in the night (as it will) &
the family that eroded as some do &

the marriage that was doomed & the evil that kids do to one another &

if you remember to tell this story as it was told,

I will send you a letter with a number & a key & when you find what
you are looking for

maybe you will remember me.

wears white & weeps blue tears down her thin cheeks & and her
silver hair is a nest of chickadees &

around her neck from a silver chain a miniature black cage
where a white cricket lives &

in her heart there's a hole that has never been filled & in her
mouth words she will never speak but

chews them day by day until they are the color of white paste
that will be her meal for the night.

The woman in the window cannot find her way in the dark &
depends on the moon & the shadows it casts

to make a path for her to come & go & in the day she is
motionless in her chair of asphodel & weeds &

looks to the horizon like a queen waiting for her lost consort &
when I see her, as I often do, I wave &

she offers a rare smile & I see her teeth are strong & her eyes
turn bright as the darkest stars.

V

Concert w/Laundry & Lemon Tree

Concert w. Laundry & Lemon Tree

For: Christopher Williams

She hangs out her wash: girdle, blouse, panties . . . In the wings a small dog with a big mouth / We'd likely feed him to the pigs.

The drummer murmurs a lazy tune, stretches sound like a rubber over an octave or an octoroon.

The Blues comes to Torrijos 68. This is no time to worry the future. Open the door to the next chapter: Climb inside your machine.

& It's beat surrounds us: hissing, undulating, whispering / a hoarse echo from the throat of the drum.

The black bass hounds & whimpers / . . . turned loose / Peeks in every rat hole to roust the sleeping guitar.

She takes down the laundry: panties first & girdle & his shirts & . . . The dog is quiet. Smells the rutting pigs. Drags its tail. Waits.

The lemon tree was planted 10 years ago. Its gnarled trunk & branches testify to its earnest wish for life.

The ensemble merges in a cacophony of scattered cymbals & ruptured strings. A bell rings / The lovers kiss

Time to read the pulse / Register the awakening of the blood / Time to Go on.

A track lined with waiting trains & overhead a flying swan in pursuit of a three-legged pony.

Two people at dinner slicing through the center of a rubber tire within which they think you see a train moving.

In another frame (pause for our handful of popcorn) we see a glossy rendering of a naked man & woman embracing / their faces clocks &

in the next (we pass quickly through the gallery) a bearded manikin with breasts has been dressed in the sailor-suit of a toddler.

(wait . . .)

A dancer with one normal leg & one wooden leads her partner in a Tango while an icy lake

thaws in the rain & fish, once asleep at the bottom, swim leisurely to the surface, join their small fins & dance too.

(& now . . .)

In slow motion, its linked wheels turning & the mammoth hulk wheezes & coughs & belches smoke & *(at last)* takes the rails in its mouth &

strides away . . . a tiny speck on the horizon dangling a
grotesque hand that waves in our camera's eye:

Bye - Bye / Bye - Bye / Bye - Bye.

open to air & swarms of bees . . . & the rambunctious donkey with
his hair between its teeth. Him

the man you witnessed last week in Jerome's bar & later @
Anthony's Pharmacy. The man

with coal for eyes & vinegar under his tongue.

When you think you've see him again he's gone / hunting, they
say / scrounging for his dead wife, we're told. & now the donkey

exhales his hair & skin / scattering what remains like stitches in the fog.

The Red Wall

1
Somewhere in the mist a woman waits for the man who agonizes over
the loss of his Chinese cat & the princess carrying water.

The woman has waited for years to hear footsteps from
her Moscow childhood & as the man playing the violin passes for

the last time she follows & declines to leave a message for those who come
each day to bathe her & cook her meal & she neglects too

the nightmare of fire & rooms without walls & her mother's cries &
will only recount her number & how long it takes to bake a loaf of bread.

2
As his houses fall to ruin & his neighbors move to the suburbs (specks of
red & black on the horizon) he fills the void with a hint of white:

doves flying & blue riders in uniform carrying guns & a message for his
wife to lock the windows & a smudge of blood

where he hurtled the last fence.

After: ***Kandinsky:*** *The Dissolution of Form*

Pumpkins

He relished pumpkins. The full-round-juicy look of them & savored an occasion to delicately remove just one small triangulated piece:

that plump sliver of fur & feathers & seeds . . . all the markings of lunch with his lover who requests a baguette & time to be naked

with grapes & surrounded by men of the street smoking or passing by as she heats their lunch in her oven &

he offers his last judgment of reasonable things: eye-glasses, shoes, bellows, candles . . . all the detritus of the world & why

he must, as her lover, decline & recline under her heel / under her blue skin to tender respect & appreciate the subtle swelling of her cleft

like a ration of that poaching pumpkin all full & round & juicy & soon to be served.

After: The paintings of ***Jean Hélion***

No need to kiss me back, she said & turned toward him &
slapped his face . . . &

no mention of that afternoon that night or that summer when
fireflies rose & fell like tongues in the dark &

they took each other's hand into the barn & the rubber he
couldn't find until the last.

That summer when the butterflies & owls fought for dominion &
a seed passed her lips & back to his

like swallowing the curds & whey of nursery rhymes when the
lightening hit & the squall tossed the boats &

the barn went up in smoke & her name had changed for the
better & his too for all she knew or wanted.

***

I've never loved anyone else, he said & slipped his hand under her
skirt when the moon was full & you could see across the lake &

hear the lowing of the loons & the pitch of the bats & her days
were numbered & so were his

playing it close to the vest & drawing down a flush to the ten &
she whipped out her jack &

left him fumbling for his chips & nights to fill with frogs &
solitaire.

***

If I return your ring it doesn't mean it's over & he walked home
in the dark

where Shirley was waiting with her hand out & a long rope for
him to pull her in.

. . . so many . . . & death awaits the eager & the rash . . .

Welcome the glow of a yellow Chanterelle with its fissures &
flutes & the bulbous Boletus & honeycombed Morels – musty,
illusive & rare &

the Saffron Milkcap – stained orange with its stippled stream of
veins & a hint of moss & the hearty Shitaki & delicate Wood-ear
& Oyster

but

beware the red-tinged & scaly Amanitas whose noxious sleep
awaits the fool with his hand in the wrong & a Death Angel

who will pierce your memory & harvest your mind & the
Muscarine whose first bite will slit a liver to shreds.

& now you must select the young

& dry & slice [not too thin] your choice & heat [not too hot] your
skillet & garlic & oil & salt & pepper & toss

with a dash of a dry white wine in a quick sauté & spread on a
bed of rice & roasted onions &

savor the succulent skin of the earth.

& Then Came Pigeons

New York City - Winter 2005

I've watched the big red headed cop

pawing the ground like a defensive end inching from the library
a monkey scratching her beefy back, a terrier

with one good eye
munching oysters in Knickerbocker's window, a bride

decked out
in white taffeta dodging traffic on Broadway, her groom

braced against-the-wall by a cameraman & his good-to-be-gone
mother-in-law.

I've tried but failed to ignore

the seven aging Chinese tourists who wear handcuffs under their
purloined lavender robes,

the mute guitar player who strums & mumbles incoherently to a
gaggle of dog walkers in Washington Square &

the ubiquitous pigeons

picking there way through this morning's fog / each pinioned louse
a test, each scabrous toe another nail in our anonymous coffin.

Bodies In The Wall

There's foot in a shoe where the bricks part.
A hand further down & a dingy fringed cuff.

There's a dark spot too & the smell of urine.

There's a shred of cloth. Blue. At the joint.
If you follow the line of fine dust as we have . . .

around the corner, bordering the garden, another wall.

Here, a battered beige coat streams from a crack & a leg . . .
Inside, someone is typing & someone is fingering her harmonica.

When I stand on tiptoe I can see thumbs fumbling at the concrete
crown.

We've counted three by now & will search for the rest after
drinks & dinner.

Eric will order a ham steak with cottage fries & Sylvia cold
tongue on rye.

I'll settle for calves liver smothered in bacon & onions /reminds
me of mom & home.

Huddled in his doorway a man stares past the memory of / The Voyage Made.

The shtetl in Vilnius bears his visage / his mother's grave

long lost in time / burnt black.

Each day he makes this voyage weaving the song of a father flogged & sister left to starve.

The weight of the Diaspora has bent his back. His exhausted arms weigh against the cloth of his weathered shirt.

A woman brings him soup in a blue ceramic bowl.

She is daughter & young & cooks & cleans.

No one has recorded his history.

Today a visitor has come to question him. She raises the question of The Voyage Made & he kisses her on her warm cheek.

She writes that he is missing two fingers from his left hand & has a blue number tattooed on his left arm.

In the dark / he's often seen wandering the park / tree to tree.

Light puffs of steam like the breath of the dying float from his flaccid skin.

There is no harbor / there is no sleep / never /
sleep.

Man To Man

Where's your Jesus now?" You ask.
"Here's Jesus now." He says.

. . . sprawled & splayed & even (if it be told) silenced, this
truncated / trivialized mongrel of the street // Drugged &

naked / dusted & junked // In the can / to be canned / like a
drunken fish tamed & teeming.

His mentors & their married *Marys* prance on his bones;
up one hole & down the next – blown black & blue / cornrow

to cornhole . . . face puffed & pounded / biffed & bashed / his
used-to-be now *might-have-been* now *gone-to-the-tombs.*

Whites of his eyes glow like dimes & his teeth (row on row on
row)
ready to tear into hand or thigh.

Each ghost / a trick passing / an opportunity / lost to the crowd
in sync to the music of the thrust & punch // Jig to the giggles &

jabber to the swarm: spat upon, blat upon, shat upon / here /
folded
in his mother's robe / across her lap,

like a lamprey suckling prayers //There's sure to be more
milking done *before the night is through* . . . tra la / tra la / tra la /
tra la

After: Portraits & Heads by: ***Francis Bacon &***
Mon Genet: Dance / ***Roberto G. Alonso & Co.***

Poem as movie

1
From the dregs of a disheveled dawn the turtle sweeps the beach trumpeting & scolding his kids(as if they were his own) like a good dada.

Smoke & a door ajar.

At the edge of town the ears turns deaf & the turtle struts & barks & bellows while the spinsters all gasp & . . . ("Time for popcorn, mommy?")

The choice is . . . You versus Vice
. . . answer on page 129

2
Come away. There's much to tell.
Come away then. While the news surrounds you.

"Hurry," she said, & tries to hold back the buckling floor.

The quaking grows more vigorous until an engine comes loose & . . .

98 passengers & crew . . . The suspected bomb was . . .

The echo of annihilation. The clock askew
keeps ticking.

He has a knife - he has
a gun - he
has a
bomb . . .

As he removes his pants & finds his way to another corpse he drops the wheels on the track . . .

The arm of the crab - Hot asphalt - [Yes!]

3
Scene:

The factory at midnight / Last shift.

That's when it happens. First, the glass goes & then the . . . 'assassination'?

. . . complete with surveillance cameras & a runner running.

Evening finds the turtle swimming in the void. He flaps his wings & sails off like the spy he is & the orphan he was but never could be.

If you were to ask him he would not say 'Because I . . .' but only shrug & that would have to do.

The blood on his cheek & on the collar of his suit betrays a joy in the hunt, nothing more / nothing less.

To study naked women on the beach or dancers in the mix means a space on the sidelines.

He's used to that. Been at it for years. Plans it that way. Never apologizes. & why not?

There was a time he was involved. It didn't last. After her, he no longer seemed to bother.

These days, he practices without a net. Comes closer. Needs to be sure it's genuine.

There's a rare photo of him. Yes. Him. In army issue fatigues, an M-16 slung across his arms.

The plaque reads: "Sharpshooter – Class A". He has good eyes & patience. It's what needed.

. . . he ordered his brother killed for fucking the queen, his wife, [what else could he do?] & the common folk loved him or so they say . . . & even the maidens were keen to do him service . . .

& when the king summoned, his attendant women would gather you up & bathe you in perfumes & oils & arrange your hair & trim & polish & dote & when you were ready they'd lift you into the day & pass you on to the captain of the guard who'd pass you on to the Minister of State & then to the place in the hall reserved for gifts & so you will be & Pedro the King shall see you blessed & send you to mark the peace between the African & Spanish states . . .

& so we are told . . . she went willingly & bold in her loose white gown & stood with eyes cast down admiring an especially ornate design in the tile at her feet & the other & younger girl with wet blue eyes quivered a bit in the heat of the moment & then they were led to their respective lords who would that night change their circumstance & names & marry them & when disposed again & again . . .

Seville, Spain 1999 / 2000

At War

In times of peace the sons will bury their fathers.
In times of war fathers bury their sons.

Thucydides

A young boy has rummaged for scraps of wood & nailed them to approximate the shape of an AK 47 automatic rifle.

His (soon-to-be army issue) web-belt
a single string he's slung across his back

will have to do (as the love song says)
until the real thing comes along.

***

There's a farmer wandering the roads of Rwanda with four bent scythes stretched across his back:

Death in an old disguise?

Maybe just another scavenger plying his trade?

***

Cahoots & chortling recruits parade / a pole / they've strung with the heads, hearts & testicles of the fallen.

As the maimed try to rise they flail & collide & it's then the Minotaur comes, sniffs the air & finding blood, feasts on the remains:

no bodies left to rot, no bones to store. No relics to hang on your slim altars.

***

The photographers that survive are always suspect:

> "Where were you when he was shot?" "Where were you when the tanks rolled in?"
>
> "Where were you when she was shattered by the mines?"
>
> "Where? *Where...*? You dare to ask."

Here. In the trench. In the trench we've scooped from sand & broken plates,

where we've been trapped in a rain of blood & shredded skin & once a leg & even arms & when we can,

we run with the stench & the stuff that clings & my film & . . .

***

If not me than who?

Who will bury this desiccated corpse / already a meal for the buzzards that hover here?

The joke that passes says, "If you steal from these well-meaning janitors you will be the first to be swept up in your next life."

I'm inclined to pass & walk away . . . & yet,
why not these birds?   I mean . . .

***

In the end / there is always / memory

The red color of the flag that hangs on death's wagon or drapes the box where Jamie sleeps

is the last your country-men & women will ever know of the blood that was spilled here.

History is packed with irony & contradiction. Don't expect sustenance. Rather, a snack to oblige & send you blithely on you way.

Never.
Look back.

The cabinet is empty / There's nothing left to claim.

***

Each drop in the bucket anticipates another soldier down.

No matter.

There are always more buckets & more bodies to be tossed.

& if it's one drop at a time /
one drop at a time it shall be.

So, it is said, by the shaman & the priests

who relish the last corpse / as if it were truly the body of hope brought here to be resurrected

or not.

CCCB (Catalunya Cultural Center Barcelona) September 2004

1 - Going in Circles

He walks from one unknown corner to the next / scattering notes
to the cross town bus & a park he's only read about

where rivers converge & a new animal ? baboon ? butterfly caresses
the Weeping Willow.

A man ? his age pushes a baby carriage across the bridge banging a pot lid against his head.

A woman escorts him strumming a guitar & shouting random insults in his one good ear: *rummy - dunce - laggard - punk . . .*

Only the baby is silent in its purple robes.
The sun is dying.

He eats his apple on the river bank /
counts the bodies as they pass.

2 - The Road

is lined with hand-hewed poles / Each with its own cadet bagged & labeled.
Each addressed to mom @ home. Each named for dad's old clan.

When the orders are given the poles are moved to the next junction.
Right or left / up the road or down / it doesn't matter.

Those who wait in the wings pay their fair & equal share.
It's tradition here.

The man who sees to their unveiling is blind.
No records are kept beyond day one

& those are repeated each day in each journal.
The nonchalant relatives do not read.

It has yet to matter.

1
A liquid kiss falls like hot wax
on the barrel chest
of the scribe

paid to recount encounters
between the restless
& the bold:

A man with a gun & a woman with a sword guard the
entrance
as if entranced or / in a trance.

The army moves its queen & takes their Bishop hostage.
The church remains
trapped

like so many dogs yapping for flesh & hemlock
laced with acid.

O come all ye faithful. Join the procession to the market for
wives /
[a later rendition of smoke gets in your eyes].

Ship's horn in the fog / The echo of blasting caps.

Beware lost children. Beware excavations.
Learn to settle for sand & mirrors.

2
Darkness overcomes the traveler . . . & thirst.

One recounts tales of anxiety & assassination. Another, the
taking
of the dentist from his country home:
3 kids, a dog, wife . . .
& the slaughter.

3
. . . still another: the making of blood pudding from what's left / scavengers among the carpets, micro-waves & refrigerators:

"Leave your knapsack at the door. It'll be safe. Trust me.
You have no choice."

Only the willing will. So it is said.
They too are measured for the box.

& another says: That Box? Yes. That. Box.

When opened, well, we know the tales of hubris & avarice & the scorched earth . . . shuffling through fields of fine grey sand that are the powdered bones.

4
In the dream that follows two people want to love each other but have forgotten how:

Where the river bisects the city.
Where the willow dips to the passing water.
Where the blanket has been spread.
Where she naps while he stares into the night.

First comes the Magpie with its nagging tales of deceit:

You were with her. Say it. Tell . . .
You were with him. Say it. Tell . . .

& the canny Camel:

There was never a 'her' or a 'him' but there were memories &
who can recover from those.

In time, the Lioness drags her dinner across a slick patch & winks:

> Spare us your grief.
> There's plenty to go around.

5

Wind along the wall &
petals fall
lacing

the walk with stitches:
orange & lavender /
butter & breath.

He worries his knuckles & studies her face.
When he looks again
she's gone.

The hollow moon has slipped away.

It's a long drive back but somehow they make it.
If not together then.
Alone.

Cimetiere du Pere Lachaise – Paris, France – July 5, 2005
Lilacs, lichen, the stiff residue of a fallen egg / how cold the stone against a thigh…

With official map in hand, they track the wake of the curious, the hunters of families & those who've come to pay

homage to their mentors whose unique lives composed a distinct allure: Frederick / Marcel / Edith / Gertrude / Oscar . . .

Unrehearsed they're startled to find themselves lost in a reverential state & even speak in whispers.

*

In the upper garden there're tributes to the Free French partisans & tributes to the outcasts of Buchenwald, Dachau & Auschwitz:

sculptures of exhausted bodies, iron bones stripped of skin that speak of the waste & carnage they saw before they fell.

& these two, alone inside their precious skins, shudder under this guise of evil & resolve to honor the implied demand: "Never Forget."

*

Muscles tense & a bite at the back of the throat, they face their ride home together but apart /

this is the day she tells him she will go on alone.

The Woman On The Bench

is elderly, black & alone. She wears a flowered hat & flowered
dress & carries her bible close to her breast. With one eye

she watches kids chasing frogs in the pond & with the other
scours the mist that hovers above that field in the Alabama

of her youth where she claimed her first kiss & later with
Abraham left a hint of blood in the grass & now

a turtle has surfaced & a brave young girl has trapped it in her
hands & Alabama rings with the rapid snap of the whip &

hollow echo of the club & now blood flows more freely & the
road north closes behind her & none are left to follow &

no one here to welcome her home.